With best wi

Bill Lomas 1988

FLOWERS AT THE ROYAL

by

John W. Bailey

GRESHAM BOOKS

Published by	:	*Mary V. Green*
Typography by	:	*Vera M. Taggart*
Printed by	:	*Burgess & Son*

The Royal Agricultural Society of England holds its annual farming trade show at the Nation Agricultural Centre, Stoneleigh, in Warwickshire, in July each year. Over 180,000 visitors atter the four day Royal Show, including over 10,000 from abroad. The flower element within T Royal Show includes many trade stands plus over 200 flower arrangements in the 12 classes. T spacious Flower Gardens with their ample catering facilities provide a social focus for visitors, addition to being home for one of the most popular flower shows in England.

The Stoneleigh Flower Garden during the 1983 Royal Show.
Below: the interior of the marquee and arrangements from various classes in the competition.

The National Federation of Women's Institutes holds its finals for the Huxley Cup each year at The Royal Show. Over thirty counties participate and the Huxley Cup is later presented at the Annual General Meeting, held at the Albert Hall in the summer. The N.F.W.I. have long been strong supporters of The Royal Show and, in particular, its flower component.

THE ROYAL SHOW

The Royal Agricultural Society of England was founded in 1838 by a group of landowners who wished to improve the nation's farming techniques by sharing their knowledge. The first show was held at Oxford the following year and attracted over 20,000 visitors. Subsequently, The Royal Show, as it became, moved to a different part of the country each year, with an all-time record attendance of over 242,000 at Newcastle in 1956. In the early sixties it became apparent that a permanent site was required and Stoneleigh was selected. The attendance at The Royal Show is now averaging 200,000 visitors.

THE FLOWER COMPETITIONS STEWARD – MRS R.T. GODBER, J.P.

Candida Godber comes from a Bedfordshire farming background. After leaving school her love of nature was furthered by taking a degree in Botany at London University, after which she worked as an Information Scientist for Unilever. Her introduction to The Royal Show was in 1961 when she helped her future husband, Richard Godber, with the National Farmers' Union market produce display at Cambridge. They were married a year later and now have two daughters and a son. For many years the flower competitions had been organised by Kathleen Robinson. When, in 1978, she suddenly became unable to continue, due to ill health, Candida Godber, at very short notice, took over the reins and has organised this event ever since. Not only does she help her husband run their farm and the Garden Centre at Willington, managed in conjunction with the Frost Group, but she is also a Justice of the Peace and a member of the Oxford Prison Board. As a person who puts much back into the community, it was typical of Candida that, when the Little Linford village church suddenly needed an organist, she filled that breach too, on an organ that needs not only musical fingers but strong legs to keep up the pressure in the bellows.

Richard Godber is a strong supporter of the R.A.S.E. and has been a Council Member for 14 years. He chairs the Planning & Works and Horticultural Committees and organises the Flower Show. He is the son of a former Minister of Agriculture, the late Lord Godber.

Hon. Richard Godber showing H.R.H. Princess Alice, The Duchess of Gloucester around the Flower Show.

THE 1983 ROYAL SHOW FLOWER COMPETITION JUDGES

Chief Judge — Mary D. Graves

Like so many keen flower arrangers, Mary Graves has always lived an active life. For many years she was a Governor of the Henrietta Barnett School in Hampstead Garden City, where she herself was educated. She was also Mayoress of Hendon whilst her husband was Mayor. Stephen Graves J.P., the Upper Bailiff of the Worshipful Company of Weavers of the City of London, has always taken a keen interest in his wife's career in flower arranging. He helped her found Hampstead Garden Suburb Flower Arranging Club, of which Mary is now the founder Life President. She is also Vice President of three other flower clubs, and, on the national scene, is Vice President of the London & Overseas Area of NAFAS. For many years she served on the Council of NAFAS, being Chairman from 1973 to 1975, and has recently become their National President. Well known throughout Britain as a demonstrator, judge and adjudicator, she has often been enlisted to judge shows and competitions in many parts of the world, including the Floralies in Belgium. Mr and Mrs Graves have a daughter, a son, and now two grandchildren. They live outside Norwich.

Mary Graves has kindly written an article for this book on judging flower shows; see page 25.

NAFAS — The National Association of Flower Arrangement Societies of Great Britain — was founded by Mrs Mary Pope, OBE, VMH, of Dorchester in 1959. It has now grown to over 1,000 clubs and societies in 20 Area Associations, and has more than 100,000 members. It is affiliated to the Royal Horticultural Society and to the National Council of State Garden Clubs of America, Ikebana International and specialist flower societies. International affiliates to NAFAS include clubs and societies in the Bahamas, Belgium, Bermuda, Canada, Cyprus, Eire, the Fiji Islands, France, Gibraltar, Jamaica, Kenya, Malawi, Malta, Monaco, Natal, New Zealand, Northern Ireland, Peru, South Africa, St Lucia and Zimbabwe. NAFAS has raised nearly £3,000,000 for charity, in addition to stimulating a widespread interest in, and enthusiasm for, flower arranging.

Associate Judge at The Royal — Bill Lomas

A NAFAS National Demonstrator and National Judge, and also winner of many awards including the Diplome d'Honneur at Monaco in 1971, and the coveted Garden Flower Trophy at the NAFAS National Competitions in 1973, Bill was also a finalist in the Midland Bank Competition for National Flower Arranger of the Year in 1976. He is Chairman of the Cheshire Area of NAFAS, and helped form two clubs in Cheshire, the Frodsham & District Flower Club and the Mid-Cheshire Flower Club. Bill is the past President of the Knutsford & District Flower Club. Now living just outside Knutsford, his garden is open to societies during the summer months.

Carolynn Harrison

FIRST PRIZE

Class 5 – Boxed Border

Carolynn's superb towering display suggested that a slender oval frame would be appropriate. Due to the profusion of flowers and variety of leaves incorporated into her exhibit, it was necessary to provide a strong 'anchor' near the centre to hold the picture together. White *Astrantia Carniolica* was selected, then the *Statice "Pink Poker"* placed to create a surround, together with a variety of interesting leaves. Gradually the picture emerged with lots of visual interest which had to both balance and interact. The strong, small shapes provided by the *Lilium Martagon* neatly crowned both the exhibit and the subsequent picture. Notice how finally the strong repetitive shape and distinctive mauve and white colouring of the *Astrantia Carniolica*, at right looking inwards, helped to prevent the picture being visually tilted towards the large mass of shapes spreading upwards at left.

CAROLYNN HARRISON

The daughter of a hosiery manufacturer in Leicestershire, Carolynn's first entry into The Royal Show was helping her father sell his 'Indestructible Socks'. She had gone through school at St. George's Ascot, without being aware that she had much artistic ability. After marriage, one of her husband's aunts, a Miss Betty Allen, sparked off her latent talent by encouraging her to join the Rugby Floral Society in 1970. Carolynn's career in flower arranging soon took off like a rocket for she kept winning prizes everywhere. She is now a very well known figure in the marquee at The Royal almost giving birth to her second son amongst the arrangements in 1974. Fortunately she managed to delay matters until the following day, so that the show could go on. A real 'trouper' amongst the flower fraternity, with such an impressive collection of awards, including The Royal Horticultural Society's Gold Medal in 1980, it was inevitable that public demand should propel her into becoming a demonstrator in many Midland counties. To further her skill she attended the Kettering Technical College's City & Guilds Course in Flower Arrangement, earning a distinction.

Recently, Carolynn converted the granary at her three centuries old home, Woolscott Manor into a classroom where she now runs professional courses in flower arranging. She founded the Woolscott Flower Club two years ago, members from which form the nucleus of her courses now attended by over 80 enthusiasts.

In 1982, for the visit of the Pope to Coventry, Carolynn assisted in decorating the podium, and the year before, had helped to decorate Westminster Abbey for the Flower Festival. Facing her in 1984 is the challenge of taking charge of all the flower arrangements for the Royal Gala N.S.P.C.C. Centenary Ball at Shire Hall, to be attended by the Charity President, H.R.H. Princess Margaret Countess of Snowdon.

She also finds time to hunt with the Fernie and Pytchley — but then, like all top flower arrangers she has lots of energy, and in Carolynn's case this is combined with indestructible determination

Mary Heal

Mary Heal has assisted in the organisation at Stoneleigh for over eight years. The Flower Show is her particular speciality for The Royal. She co-ordinates the requirements of the Chief Flower Steward, Mrs. Godber, who organises the competitions and exhibits, with the help of a team of volunteers drawn mainly from local flower clubs. Lady Stella Harriman, the Flower Steward, has her own team of helpers who take on the considerable task of decorating the R.A.S.E. pavilions. Throughout the show they are responsible for conditioning the flowers and foliage, so that all remain as fresh as possible. Candida Godber's private army, together with Lady Harriman's, is about 50 strong. For many years the stalwarts have been Miss E. Rotherham and Mrs. C. Adams, ably assisted by Mrs. D. Reddy and Mr. K. Faulkner. To those who kept the flowers looking fresh in the sweltering heat, I am personally most grateful; without their efforts little worth pressing would have remained and this book would not have been possible.

PRESSING FLOWERS

To create a good picture the artist needs the best materials possible; so the technique of transforming a 'living' flower into the permanent 'dried' condition requires study. It is a form of process engineering, for the flower is not just being flattened but is having its internal moisture carefully leeched out leaving behind the nutrients as a 'glue' to hold the delicate structure together and fix its colour.

Inevitably, some shrinkage will occur depending upon the amount of moisture within each flower and leaf, and the colour tones will tend to darken as they become, in consequence, more concentrated. If the moisture within is removed too fast, wrinkling and possibly disintegration will take place. If the moisture is removed too slowly there is the danger of an onset of mould, particularly in a press which is not properly ventilated. The commonly-held view that a presser just places flowers into a telephone directory and lets them press for a few weeks is a fallacy, for this method, whilst sometimes giving a good result, is in fact a very unreliable approach to the task.

The only way to learn is to experiment, for flowers do vary in their moisture content and internal structure. Blotting paper is probably the best agent for removing moisture, but for some flowers a drying crystal, such as silica gel, may give you an even better result. There are all sorts of tricks you learn as you progress which assist you to achieve the best possible results out of your raw material.

The difficulty with the prize winners in the Boxed Border Class at the 1983 Royal Show, was to press the arrangements before they fell to pieces, for the weather during the show was swelteringly hot and in the marquee it was nearly tropical. Due to the devoted attention of the marquee staff the 214 different arrangements were kept reasonably spruce during the four days of the show. When it ended I rushed home with the seven arrangements and then pressed through the night. It was a close run race.

Eileen Stevens

SECOND PRIZE

The artist always faces a problem when there is a strong mass of concentrated colour, as is the case with Eileen's blue *Delphinium*. If it is placed near the middle a 'bull's eye' effect occurs and if placed too far to one side it will look odd, like the star of the show who is nearly off-stage. I started off hoping to balance the blue mass with some *Rosa Gallica* popping out at top left, whilst the eye-drawing fascinating shapes of the *Alstroemeria* gave counterbalance at the bottom of the evolving picture. However, even the subsequent inclusion of some tonally strong pink and red *Roses*, plus a scatter of *Scabious* arching up at right, failed to reduce sufficiently the strength of that mass of blue. The eventual solution was to swing the *Delphinium* to the left and place the deep red stick of *Lythrum "Rose Queen"* on the other side so as to be nearer the centre, thus setting up a colour to shape balance which helped subdue the mass of blue.

EILEEN N.M. STEVENS

Miss Stevens' family have lived in Derbyshire for over three centuries, so she has strong local roots. She probably inherited her love of the land from her grandfather and great grandfather who were both professional horticulturalists. After leaving school, she went to Bedford College for Women, but at the outbreak of war she joined the Civil Nursing Reserve. In 1941 she joined the Women's Auxiliary Air Force and was in the first draft of airwomen to go abroad, serving in Egypt and Palestine until demobilisation in 1946. She then resumed her studies, taking a B.Sc. General course in Botany, Zoology and Chemistry at Derby Technical College, whilst also maintaining her links with the Air Force in the Volunteer Reserve. Her return to full time service was delayed by ill health, but after two serious operations she re-joined the W.R.A.F. in 1956 as a Flying Officer in the Secretarial Branch. It was whilst serving at R.A.F. Wyton that her career in flower arranging began. When H.R.H. The Duchess of Gloucester visited the station to present the 58 Squadron Standard, the professional florist charged so much for decorating the Officers' Mess that Eileen was asked to "organise the flowers" for H.R.H. The Duke of Edinburgh's visit the following year. With an allowance of only £20, she sought the help of the Station workshops who fashioned six wrought iron pedestals from scrap metal, and in the Mess storeroom she discovered some old, plated entrée dishes to grace the long oak dining tables as flower containers. Her colour scheme was blue and white; she used scabious, cornflowers, carnations, delphiniums and "Bride" gladioli. Her organisation was a huge success, so she earned herself a new task within the R.A.F.

Eileen's last posting was to R.A.F. Halton where the Officers' Mess was located in the former home of Alfred Rothschild. This had a useful aspect in that the gardens of this former stately home contained an abundance of interesting foliage for her arrangements. After leaving the R.A.F. she did a teacher's course in flower arranging at S.E. Derbyshire College of Further Education and has subsequently taught the art locally in Derbyshire and Leicestershire. For many years she has decorated her local parish church and she also helps with festivals at the nearby Cheshire Home at Staunton Harold. She has been a member of the Loughborough Flower Lovers' Club for over 14 years, and five years ago she started the Castle Donington & District Flower Club. The latter now has over 100 members, and Eileen is Founder President.

PRESSED FLOWER PICTURE COMPOSITION

Out of the press, about six weeks later, comes your 'palette'. If you have ever painted in oils the problem that confronts you is basically the same — the interaction of areas of colour and shape to produce a pleasing aesthetic statement. However, the picture subject is already fixed, for you are about to commence the assembly of a whole range of shapes provided by nature. As you study the selection from the press laid out before you, creative possibilities begin to generate in the mind. It is a bit like studying the pieces of a jig-saw puzzle and wondering which will fit together. Of course you can modify the 'shapes', but not very much. Furthermore, a certain honesty is required; for to reassemble the petals of, for example, a rose to produce a flower which looks more like a daisy or some weird self-created flower, which has never existed naturally is, to my mind, dishonest. The aim surely must be to recreate nature in a lifelike manner, working into your picture a sense of movement, for flowers are seen in the mind 'dancing in the wind'.

When you look at a good flower arrangement at a show or in a church, or in a house where the hostess has some talent in that direction, you know that the composition could not be quite like that 'in the garden' due to the concentration of flower and leaf in dramatic form, but it is not too distant from the real thing, for it is nature enhanced — not distorted. Similarly, the flower picture artist strives for this same effect with his raw materials.

The pictures I have created from the Royal Show Boxed Border Class arrangements, as you can see, cannot imitate those original flower arrangements. Instead they are a recreation, each in its own right, using the same materials — but in a different form. There is an artistic linkage between these two types of art, for if you remove a flower from a good arrangement it destroys the balance of the whole. Similarly, if you do the same with one of the components of a finished flower picture, the visual harmony is lost.

No two artists will produce exactly the same result. Each flower arranger and picture maker has his own sense of what looks right. That is the charm of both art forms — your own originality harnessed into the rather haphazard quality of nature in the raw.

KEEPING FLOWERS FRESH PRIOR TO PRESSING

At a Flower Show, the attendants give the arrangements a light spray of water. Its evaporation helps to reduce the temperature of the flower and its rate of decay. The same result can be achieved, more effectively, with flowers which have been picked for pressing, if they are placed in a fridge. The flowers must be dry, so do not sprinkle them with water in the hope that this helps them to remain fresh. Never place them in a freezer, which is too cold and would destroy the flowers by freezing the moisture within the delicate internal veins. Flowers placed in a fridge last for many days, and if then sent by post arrive at their destination in a satisfactory condition for the picture maker.

Gillian Collett

THIRD PRIZE

Gillian's *Enchantment Lily* was going to be the dominant shape, come what may, and the soaring nature of its powerful impact meant it had to go high up and on the periphery of the picture at top left. To 'anchor' it, some strong leaf shapes were required, and the variegated *Cupressus* camc in handy at centre left, plus a heavy cluster of *Box Leaves* right down at the bottom of the picture. The rather dull-shaped *Solomon's Seal* leaf pointing to the right was intended to provide a springboard for interest, but as the picture developed, it got lost to view. The mass of leafy shapes which had started with a small spring of variegated *Cupresssus* pointing upwards and to the right from the left hand side curve, proved later to be too low, and in the final adjustment that centre of interest had to be canted further upwards to balance those *Enchantment Lilies* which had remained serenely supreme throughout the construction of this picture.

GILLIAN COLLETT

Gillian's delight in flowers was affectionately derived from her father when she was a child. Mr. Dyer, as a young boy, had developed a great fascination for all the plant and animal life to be found in the hedgerows of Warwickshire. There was an essay competition at school. He wrote about his absorbing hobby, winning the prize, a nature book.

His love of nature grew and much later, when he was married and had a daughter, he passed on his excitement to her whenever they went for walks in the countryside around Stratford-Upon-Avon. However, Gillian's start in flower arranging was to blossom much later, after she had grown up and got a job in an insurance office. Subsequently she elevated her sights and was to win many prizes in local flower events.

When, in 1963, The Royal Show found a permanent site in nearby Stoneleigh, Gillian became a regular competitor and in 1972 won the Bronze Medal, awarded to the second best entrant in the whole show. Married, with two grown up daughters, Gillian now finds an additional outlet for her energies in a Stratford-Upon-Avon china shop.

FLOWERS WHICH PRESS BEST

Instead of giving a long list of names, let us concentrate on the principle. Moisture must be removed at a controlled rate to leave the nutrients behind as a 'glue'. Any flower or plant with a great deal of moisture in its structure will not press well. The large orchid is so fleshy it really does not press at all, and the only way of getting some form of pressed orchid, is to iron it under layers of blotting paper, which is tedious. When all the moisture has been removed, you are left with a brown leaf devoid of its former exotic colouring.

Flowers from the tropics are probably the hardest of all to press, although I have not yet experimented with them. Tropical flowers tend to burst quickly into bloom, whereas flowers from the temperate zones take their time and are thus more hardy. To withstand the chill of a cold night and the blazing heat of high noon in mid-summer, their internal structure has developed resilience over centuries of evolution, which makes them capable of withstanding the rigours of the press. Some have a structure which present a challenge and these are the flowers with an array of small long petals not strongly affixed to the heart of the flower.

Very small flowers usually press extremely well, but care should be taken with very large petals, due to their shrinkage factor. Leaves which are thin press satisfactorily, but if they show signs of being prone to tear or fracture during picture making, give the back of them a spray of varnish, which acts as a reinforcing skin.

The above are only guidelines; experimentation is the way to learn.

THE BALANCE OF COLOUR AND SHAPE

The 'correct' balance is a matter of personal judgement, hence individual artistry. Strong tones such as red, pink, orange and blue will force themselves to the fore in a picture, so they must be arranged to balance one another. The eye of the beholder naturally tends to go to the centre of a picture, so if you place too strong a tone there you will achieve a 'bull's eye' effect, which can annoy the eye. Large masses will tend to dominate and hold the attention of the viewer, so care must be taken that masses are balanced, thus spreading the interest throughout the whole picture. The various shapes which nature provides can be either interesting or dull. If the latter, they have a use as backing for the brighter objects, and if the former, they have a role to play in heightening interest by their fascinating liveliness.

The artist must respect a certain discipline when creating a flower picture, for when completed the work should resemble nature and not be a distortion of nature. Flowers are expected to reach upwards, or bend downwards, and must appear anchored to something – not just floating about haphazardly.

To summarize, tones must be placed so that they spread interest throughout the picture and masses must be arranged to compliment the strong tones. Once this is established the fun begins with the fine tuning which then either makes the picture interesting by the intriguing blend of shape and colour, or ruins it by trying to attempt the impossible. No picture will ever be perfect, so it is best to stop adjusting when you think you have got as near perfection as is within your capability. For to keep 'chopping and changing', especially with the major masses and blobs of colour, can cause you to lose all sense of artistic direction, and thus blunder into an incomprehensible mess.

In the build-ups I have shown, you can see that very early on a theme emerges, which is then built upon. Sometimes you will get it wrong, as I have shown in the next arrangement. Then there is a natural tendency to be excessive in the hope that all will 'come out right' in the end. It will not; for if the mass and tonal balance at the outset is seriously unharmonious, then discord prevails. In such a case it is better to start again, simplifying your 'palette' and trying various background colours which may aid you to overcome the problem.

I believe many men would make flower pictures if they were not so concerned with the 'image factor'. Perhaps the marvellously funny Monty Python song about the 'weirdo' lumberjack, preys on the subconscious. I was amused that our youngest son felt it necessary to explain to his friends at St. Mary's Hospital, where he is studying medicine, that his father was 'into floral engineering'. I expect they all believe that I am doing something acceptable, such as decorating the motorways!

Josephine Sansome

VERY HIGHLY COMMENDED

Josephine gave the artist a lucky "break" because her interesting selection of greyish leaves, which included some *Santolina Chamaecyparissus*, allowed a well balanced framework to be erected for the subsequent design. The strong pink *Carnation* was useful to sweep the attention upwards to balance the visually strong pull downwards of her *Rosa Cardinal de Richelieu* and *Charles de Mills* deep red roses. The picture was so easy to create, that some experimentation was attempted to investigate what would happen if the centre background was reduced in tone. The arrangement was removed and then using a can of matt white oil paint, marketed for modellers, I gave a light touch of white in the middle and reassembled the picture. The deepening of interest thus produced, caused me to wonder what would happen if the amount of white was increased and some matt blue also sprayed onto the picture, reducing the too thrustful mottled blue cotton cloth. Alas, I overdid the white in the middle, almost drowning out the texture of the cloth, so it was a question of learning from too much exploratory enthusiasm.

JOSEPHINE SANSOME

Married to a landowner/farmer, with a daughter Sarah, but not of a farming background, Josephine Sansome is a vivacious and lively personality. A personal tragedy started her interest in flower arranging, for she lost her son when he was eight. Afterwards, she found solace and then a creative outlet in busying herself in this art form. Her biggest challenge so far has been organising a very successful Flower Festival at the 13th Century family church of St. James, Ansty. She has exhibited regularly at The Royal for the past 11 years, often being Commended or Highly Commended. Her interest in flower arranging led to her helping to run the Flower Shop in the huge Walsgrave General Hospital at Walsgrave, Coventry. This hospital has over 1200 beds, and, with the assistance of 50 volunteers, Josephine decorates the reception areas at Christmas. Her resourceful and jolly determination makes Josephine the ideal person with whom to share any difficult situation.

FRAMES FOR FLOWER PICTURES

The rectangular or square frame lends itself well to the normal picture, for the artist is inferring that it is a view of something which did not just end at the boundary of the frame. However, with a floral picture an angular frame does not look right. An oval frame is more in sympathy with the subject matter – flowers. The reason for this is that the floral picture is really half design and half picture, and, due to their supple nature, flowers look better 'on the curve'. A frame should enhance a picture, not detract from the subject-matter by being too fussy or gross in shape. A good frame is merely a decorative surround, drawing attention to the picture hanging on the wall.

Some flower picture artists basically work with petals and leaves. For them, the normal frames on the market are suitable, being designed for those who work on canvas or paper. My pressing techniques have developed towards the 'whole flower'. These pictures need more deeply recessed frames, so I now make my own.

CHOICE OF THE BACKGROUND MATERIAL AND ITS COLOUR

There are two basic choices for backgrounds, either art paper or material. Most flower picture artists start on paper then progress to some form of material, such as silk or velvet, because the range of colour tones available are so much wider. A material with a slight pattern can give an interesting result, but one must be careful to avoid a pattern which thrusts itself forward and thus dominates, the pressed flowers. Materials with a sheen should be avoided for the same reason.

When selecting a background, colour can make all the difference to your picture. If chosen correctly the background will set off the subject matter and also assist in overall colour blending. In general it is best to opt for either a dark or light background when first beginning with this art form, for then you master the silhouette aspect of backgrounds. The mid-tone range adds certain complications, for the subject matter can become lost in it. However, once experience is gained, the fun is to try all sorts of variations, thus extending your creative horizons.

In the picture made from Josephine Sansome's flowers, you can see that a blue cotton cloth was used, then a tonal variation introduced with a light spray of matt white. A further experiment was made with a few deft sprays of matt blue onto the background material. The possibilities are almost limitless, and one is helped by so many varieties of spray paint being on the market.

Women are probably more colour conscious than men, for even as young girls they begin a lifelong study of what to wear. Being artistic, the female of the species is a master of blending colour, which puts her streets ahead of the poor male who only dares decorate himself with bright colours in the form of medal ribbons. The male recognises that he is visually only a prop for the female and for official occasions dresses in black or grey so that her beauty is enhanced by the range of colours she chooses. I think this is right and proper, but in certain fields, such as flower arranging or picture making, the male is struggling along behind her. Perhaps without knowing it, she has been studying colour from an early age and subconsciously knows just what balances. Women tend to make better interior designers than men and when visiting an art gallery may often see a picture more as an interaction of colour and shape than as a statement. They are probably also thinking, "that would go nicely with the curtains in the drawing room". However, men should not give up hope, we are at least quite handy with a shovel!

The flower picture artist has such an advantage over those who use oil or water colour paints. It is part art and part layout craft. It has a linkage with the work done by flower arrangers, who construct in three dimensions, experimenting freely. The flower picture artist can also experiment, for he has full control of his background colour and texture. He does not need to stick anything down until he is finally satisfied. He can raid the kitchen for a wide pie knife and transfer his picture in sections on to an entirely new background, or different backgrounds and spray paints as well. It is surprising why more people do not take up this art form as a hobby; you do not have to be very talented, just full of optimistic perseverance.

Jean Daymond

HIGHLY COMMENDED

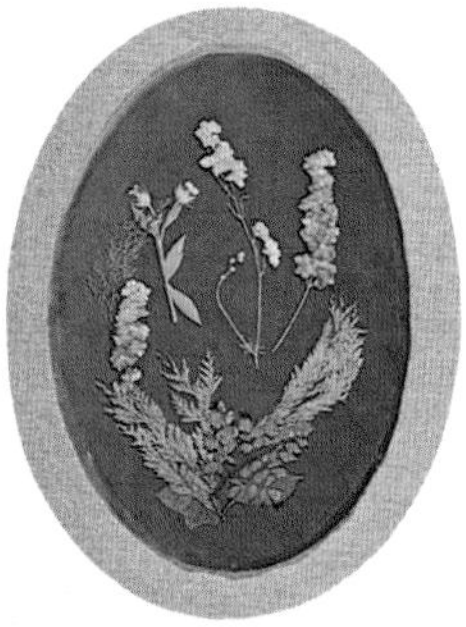

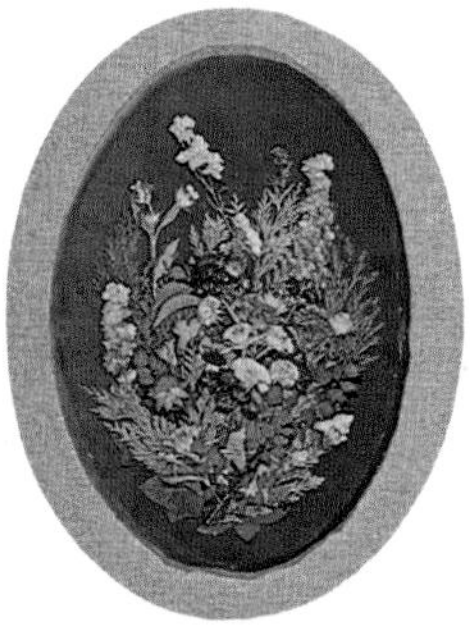

A beautiful exhibit but one which was bound to present a problem. The strong pink towering *Delphinium* blooms were dominant and there was little available to suppress their strength. Various possibilities were tried but the picture tended to get 'overloaded'. A fresh start, using a simpler approach was tried, as well as various background colours and textures. However, it is with regret that I must confess that I did not do justice to Jean's fine exhibit.

JEAN DAYMOND

Married with a son age 18, Jean has been a keen and talented flower arranger for over 16 years. Whilst living near Stoneleigh she was Treasurer and later Chairman of the Kenilworth Flower Club, and assisted in the decorations of the new Coventry Cathedral for its consecration. She has taken part in the National Competition at Trentham Gardens near Stoke-on-Trent in addition to many floral competitions in the Midlands, winning many prizes. For several years Jean was employed by the De Montfort Hotel at Kenilworth as their florist, and during this period decorated The Royal Pavilion at Stoneleigh on two occasions. Five years ago after moving to Mollington, Jean joined the Banbury Floral Club, and is now its Secretary. She is much sought after by Womens' Institutes as a lecturer in Floral Art, and has a full time job as Secretary/P.A.

ORGANISATION OF SHOWS

Shows do not just happen, they have to be planned a long time in advance with meticulous care A large show, such as The Royal, has an enormously varied number of ingredients. Each must be married together so that 'on site' a harmonious organisation is created for the benefit of the public. Traders are really only interested in their particular business and to some extent each exhibitor feels the same. This requires the organisers to have a strong sense of leadership, or chaos would ensue.

There is another factor if the public are going to enjoy the show. It is hard to describe, but it is very important. Let us call it the 'spiritual factor'. A memorial service has it naturally; it is the "raison d'être". A dog show like Crufts has it due to its long history. The Royal Show, I believe, has it for a variety of reasons. Farming is often a lonely occupation: so meeting once a year creates a natural 'spiritual factor' for those who work on the land and have a rapport with nature, as well as a need to update their knowledge of agricultural technology.

An organiser must never take the 'spiritual factor' for granted. It must be nurtured by sound administration and the ability to foresee problems. They must have the capability to overcome the inevitable ones that arise with both sense and much good humour.

My Naval background suggests that there is a marked similarity between shows and amphibious landings. Over a few days, a multitude of various forces are going to suddenly arrive and be funnelled into a small area. They will disembark a vast array of equipment and personnel, followed by a huge army of visitors. To ensure that all goes well, a good 'beachmaster' is required. In my experience the officials at the National Agricultural Centre fulfil this task to perfection.

JUDGING AT FLOWER SHOWS

by Mary D. Graves

By courtesy of the Peterborough Evening Telegraph.

To be invited to judge a show is a great compliment, but it carries a heavy responsibility, not only to the promoters of the show, but also to the competitors who spend so much time, money and effort on their exhibits, and, naturally, expect high standards from a qualified judge.

Most Societies require their show to be judged according to the NAFAS Handbook, Schedule of Definitions, 7th Edition 1982, but the judge must always check the Show Committee's schedule to ascertain if any changes have been incorporated for any of the classes.

The first essential point to consider in any arrangement is whether the plant material does predominate over all other components in the exhibit. Then one begins to study the arrangement as a work of art, which includes the basic principles of design, such as its scale, proportion, balance, rhythm and contrast. The interpretation of a theme is most important, especially these days when schedules have become so imaginative and competitors so clever.

Regretfully, one finds certain faults which occur in nearly every show. These must be taken into consideration, points such as creased drapes and damaged foliage, an over abundance of accessories, or an accessory out of scale with the rest of the exhibit. Sometimes you find badly printed title cards, or startlingly white cards when a muted colour would have harmonised so much better, and the actual positioning of a card can make quite a difference. On the other hand, some exhibitors show great ingenuity with their titles, using beautiful lettering on wood or stone.

The use of comment cards by Judges is now generally recognised as helpful to the exhibitor and generates interest for visitors to the show, particularly for exhibits which, at first sight, the public might regard as worthy of a prize. It is essential that the comments of the Judge are tactful and give kindly and constructive criticism, thus offering the exhibitor encouragement. Where the Judge feels doubt, the benefit should always be given to the exhibitor.

It is said that a Judge is only popular with the 1st Prize Winner in each class. However, it is always most reassuring and satisfying when one later hears that the general consensus of opinion was in agreement with the decision of the Judge. It is a very real pleasure for a Judge to award a prize to an outstanding exhibit, with that elusive quality of distinction we all strive to achieve.

Audrey Daniels

COMMENDED

The problem in this picture was to create a design which could incorporate the strong tone and shape of the *Penstemon.* Flowers with a repetitive shape will always tend to dominate, rather like a recurring note in a symphony. I overcame the problem by making the *Penstemon* face outwards, containing it with a pointed leaf. Using the strong leaf shape of *Helleborus* on the other side of the picture, provided a balance. A small white flower, near the centre, draws the eye inwards.

Winifred Rumsey

COMMENDED

Wynn's towering *Lavatera*, together with her wide selection of flowers: *Alstroemeria, Helenium, Armeria*, pink *Veronica, Tellima* and the marvellous curling leaf of *Polystichum*, made this picture easy to create. The shapes and tones provided a natural rhythm in the construction. Note how at a little above centre, some small white flowers help to offset the strong upward visual pull of the *Lavatera*, complimenting and reducing the impact of of the rust red *Alstroemeria* at left centre. The mauve red *Tellima* at bottom right helps draw the eye downwards. Selecting flowers with interesting shapes balances the powerful *Lavatera* at the top. The dark background creates a more dramatic effect than a light one.

AUDREY DANIELS

London born and bred, Audrey's family moved to the Midlands when she was in her teens. On leaving school she became a tracer with a Patent Agent. She met her husband in a church choir in Sutton Coldfield, where his father was the organist. Music was to become a strong thread in the Daniels' subsequent married life, for they have always sung together in choirs and local operatic societies. It was through assisting with the floral decorations in church that Audrey entered the field of competitive flower arranging, when they lived at Kenilworth. With Stoneleigh nearby, she exhibited at The Royal in 1980, and was awarded a Commended. She has exhibited regularly since then, along with her younger daughter, who has a strong tendency to upstage her mother and has won several awards. Her husband was recently promoted to be Manager of the Midland Bank in Ludlow so they have moved to Worcestershire, where they are putting down roots, both vocal and horticultural.

WINIFRED RUMSEY

Married to a farmer, Wynn grew up in the Staffordshire and Shropshire border country. As a child she was taken regularly to The Royal Show, before it found a permanent site at Stoneleigh. Wynn's interest in flower arranging started 7 years ago when her daughter persuaded her to attend a course at Trysull near Wolverhampton, run by Denis Granger. The two novices had quite a shock for they had signed up for an advanced course, but they struggled to keep up and enjoyed it. Fired with enthusiasm, Wynn has since taken part in many floral shows and has won the Claverley Chrysanthemum Society Rose Bowl for the past three years. Her husband Alan persuaded her to enter The Royal Show in 1983, and she was delighted with the result. Alan and Wynn are a very energetic couple, for not only does he farm but was also, for many years, a licensed racehorse trainer. He is now one of the top breeders of Border Terriers and, together with Wynn, runs boarding kennels with a capacity for 80 dogs. The kennels are further down the hill from their home, which has a marvellous view of the Welsh mountains. They have two daughters and a son.

John W. Bailey — Author

The author lived the first eight years of his life in Long Island, U.S.A. The family returned to England in 1934. He joined the Royal Navy in 1943 and spent most of his career 'pulling down the flag' as Great Britain shed her Empire. His last job before retirement was to set up a Coast Guard for the then recently independent island of Jamaica. He became an international Sales Executive with the Plessey Company and later a Defence Advisor for a Marine Consultancy, before entering exhibition work, first with a trade association and then with a publishing firm.

John Bailey has always been interested in painting and sculpture, carving and drawing. He tended to be a 'Jack-of-all-trades-and-master-of-none' until a friend suggested he take over his hobby/business making brides' bouquets into floral pictures. In this field he found a fulfilling spare-time outlet for his creativity.

This book project was born in the marquee at Stoneleigh, a few weeks after the author had suddenly and unexpectedly been made redundant. Due to his age, he was unlikely ever to get another job. The project was almost stillborn for 13 publishers subsequently turned it down. Some of the major publishing houses suggested he try a smaller publishing company. He spread his net in that direction and immediately had offers from two firms.

No book of this type is a solo effort, for it requires the enthusiastic co-operation of many to launch it. The author soon found that flower arrangers were a most helpful group of people. The nature of their art form presumably sorts out the 'real' people of quality from the phoney, for there can be no room for a silly prima donna in a crowded marquee, where, with an armful of flowers, the arrangers work against the clock to produce something visually splendid.

John Bailey was fortunate that his publisher found a superb printer for the book, which was then written around the capabilities of their Heidelberg Speedmaster press.

POSTSCRIPT

Throughout the production of this book, I have been encouraged by the help of many. As I created the pictures my mind kept going back to the last sentence in the article on Judging by Mary Graves, for it is the essential truth of what flower arranging is all about. It is also true for the artist — that search for the elusive quality of perfection. *J.W.B.*

BOUQUET ART OF J.W. BAILEY

The spiritual rapport a bride has with a bouquet is deep. This rapport may go right back to the long, slow evolutionary period of mankind as a cave dweller, for all a cave maiden had to mark her special day was a posy of wild flowers.

The Victorians became interested in the pressed flower picture and often a bride's bouquet was transformed by this method into a picture to grace her new home. However, the invention of photography eclipsed this form of lasting memento and the Wedding Album became the bride's principal reminder of her day. Recently, the desire to preserve the bouquet in picture form has revived, perhaps because, with so many guests taking photographs and now even video film, the young bride yearns for some memento that really is — exclusive to herself.

The rose
aristocrat of flowers

From a
country garden

Busting out all over
in June

In Chaucer's footsteps
from the Pilgrims' Way

THE ROYAL SHOW FLORAL COMPETITION, 1983

CLASS 1	–	FLYING HIGH	A modern exhibit. No accessories. Space 2'6" wide and 2' deep.
CLASS 2	–	WINTER STORE	An exhibit featuring dried plant material. No additional backgrounds may be used. Space 2' wide and 2' deep.
CLASS 3	–	'GREENSLEEVES'	An exhibit featuring foliage. No accessories, and no additional backgrounds may be used. Space 2' wide and 2' deep.
CLASS 4	–	BEST OF BRITISH	An exhibit to be staged on a platform, covered with natural hessian, 1'6" from the ground, 4' wide, 3' deep. The backing natural hessian to be 6' from the ground. This class is open to Flower Arrangement Clubs, Societies, or any two individuals.
CLASS 5	–	BOXED BORDER	An exhibit from the garden. No accessories. No additional background may be used. Space 2'6" wide and 2' deep.
CLASS 6	–	BLAZE AWAY	An exhibit to be seen from all sides. Space 2'6" wide and 2' deep.
CLASS 7	–	COUNTRY FESTIVAL	A pedestal exhibit. Exhibitors to provide their own pedestal. Space 4' wide, against a backing of off-white corrugated paper 7' high.
CLASS 8	–	TEA TIME	An exhibit to be seen from all sides. Space 2'6" wide and 2' deep.
CLASS 9	–	SOUVENIR	A petite exhibit to be staged on tiered staging painted off-white.
CLASS 10	–	KITCHEN GARDEN	An exhibit. Space 3' wide and 2' deep.
CLASS 11	–	ISLAND STORY	An exhibit featuring water. Space 3' wide and 2' deep.
CLASS 12	–	A FAMOUS LANDMARK IN BEAUTIFUL BRITAIN	Open only to NFWI County Federations for the Huxley Cup Competition. An exhibit in space 3' wide and 2' deep.